W9-BYW-323

WITHDRAWN FROM
COLLECTION

An Illustrated Timeline of
TRANSPORTATION

by Kremena T. Spengler
illustrated by Eldon Doty

PICTURE WINDOW BOOKS
a capstone imprint

Special thanks to our adviser, Terry Flaherty, PhD, Professor of English,
Minnesota State University, Mankato, for his expertise.

Editor: Jill Kalz
Designer: Tracy Davies
Art Director: Nathan Gassman
Production Specialist: Sarah Bennett
The illustrations in this book were created with ink and color wash.

Photo Credits: Iakov Kalinin, Mikhail Nekrasov, Shutterstock: cozta, WDG Photo

Picture Window Books
1710 Roe Crest Drive
North Mankato, MN 56003
www.capstonepub.com

Copyright © 2012 by Picture Window Books, a Capstone imprint.
All rights reserved. No part of this book may be reproduced without
written permission from the publisher. The publisher takes no
responsibility for the use of any of the materials or methods described
in this book, nor for the products thereof.

All books published by Picture Window Books
are manufactured with paper containing at least
10 percent post-consumer waste.

Library of Congress Cataloging-in-Publication Data
Spengler, Kremena.
 An illustrated timeline of transportation / by Kremena T. Spengler ;
illustrated by Eldon Doty.
    p. cm. — (Visual timelines in history)
 Includes index.
 ISBN 978-1-4048-6661-4 (library binding)
 ISBN 978-1-4048-7019-2 (paperback)
 1. Transportation engineering—History—Chronology—Juvenile
literature. 2. Motor vehicles—History—Chronology—Juvenile
literature. I. Doty, Eldon, ill. II. Title.
 TA1149.S64 2012
 388.09—dc22
                    2011010467

Printed in the United States of America in North Mankato, Minnesota.
012012   006567R

Long ago, humans walked wherever they needed to go. They used animals to carry loads and pull carts and wagons. Over time, people created machines such as trains, ships, and airplanes to help them move faster, farther, and higher. This movement—by land, water, or air—is called transportation.

This book is written in the form of a timeline. It lists events in the order in which they happened. Important chunks of time, such as the Automotive Age, are grouped together. You don't have to read the book from start to finish (though you can if you want to). Dip in and out! Discover how transportation has changed people's lives around the world.

ANCIENT TIMES

► 6300 BC

People in the present-day Netherlands make dugout canoes from hollowed-out logs.

4000 BC

The ancient Egyptians discover how to join pieces of wood together. By joining wood, they can make larger, longer boats.

6000 BC

People in Scandinavia (present-day Denmark, Norway, and Sweden) make wooden sleds to travel on snow.

4000 BC

People in the Middle East start using animals to pull heavy loads.

3500 BC

People in Mesopotamia (present-day Iraq) invent the wheel. They use it to build simple wagons and carts.

2500 BC

The camel is tamed around this time. It helps people travel through deserts.

300 BC

Traders begin travel along the Silk Road. The road runs 4,000 miles (6,437 km) between Europe and Asia.

500 BC

Persian King Darius builds the Royal Road. It is 1,500 miles (2,414 km) of roads between the Persian Gulf and the Mediterranean Sea.

Mediterranean Sea Next Right

1500 Miles

AD 117

At its peak, the Roman Empire has 50,000 miles (80,467 km) of roads.

312 BC

The ancient Romans build the Via Appia. It is the first of a system of well-drained, stone-paved roads.

Apian Way Toll Booth

DARK, MIDDLE, AND EARLY MODERN AGES

605

Chinese workers begin building the Grand Canal system. The 1,114-mile (1,793-km) waterway is used to transport grain.

1086

Records first show the use of a compass. Chinese sailors used one at sea.

1000

Viking ships led by Leif Eriksson cross the North Atlantic Ocean. They are thought to be the first European ships to reach North America.

1373

Canal builders in the Netherlands perfect locks. Locks are the "steps" that carry ships up or down between two water levels.

1450

By this time, the Inca in Peru have built 20,000 miles (32,187 km) of roads. The roads connect 10 million people.

1485

Leonardo da Vinci designs a parachute. He later designs a flying machine with wings, an early submarine, and an early helicopter.

1673

Colonists build the Boston Post Road. This series of roads runs between Boston, Massachusetts, and New York City. The roads will become the first highways in the United States.

1457

The first smooth-riding four-wheeled coaches are built in Hungary. The design will quickly spread throughout Europe.

EXPLORING NEW MODES

1732

The first U.S. stagecoach line to serve the public opens in New Jersey.

1771

Cugnot's second steam carriage runs into a wall at about 3 miles (4.8 km) an hour. It is the world's first "car" accident.

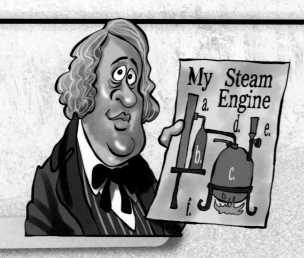

1765

Scottish engineer James Watt invents a steam engine. Steam engines will later power boats and locomotives.

1769

Frenchman Nicolas-Joseph Cugnot builds a steam carriage, an early type of automobile.

1775

Daniel Boone and a party of settlers widen an American-Indian trail (the Warrior's Path) in Tennessee and Kentucky. It becomes the Wilderness Road.

1783

On June 4, French brothers Joseph and Jacques Montgolfier fly the first hot air balloon.

1779

A short canal is built in Quebec, Canada. It is the first canal with locks in North America.

1797

Some roads in Shropshire, England, are switched to iron rails. Horses pull wagons along these rails as an early form of railroad.

1776

American David Bushnell builds the Turtle, an early submarine.

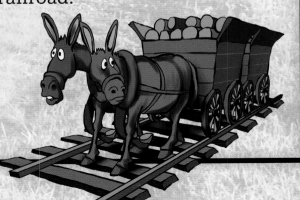

POWERED BY STEAM

1804

Englishman George Cayley flies the first unpiloted glider.

1811

Robert Fulton and Robert R. Livingston start a steamboat service on the Mississippi River.

February 21, 1804

The first working steam locomotive runs in England. It hauls five coal cars along 10 miles (16 km) of track.

August 17, 1807

The first reliable steamboat sails up the Hudson River from New York City to Albany. Built by Robert Fulton, it's called the *Clermont*.

1815

John McAdam, a Scottish engineer, invents a new way to build roads in Great Britain. The basics of his layered, hard surface method are still used today.

January 5, 1818

The *James Monroe* sails from New York City to Liverpool, England. It is the start of the world's first transatlantic service.

1818

German engineer Rudolph Ackermann makes a way to steer horse-drawn carriages. The steering method is still used in modern vehicles.

1816

Baron Karl von Drais, a German engineer, makes an early type of bicycle. Basically, it's a bike without pedals or gears.

LAYING TRACK

September 27, 1825

The Stockton & Darlington Railway opens in England. It is the world's first steam railroad.

1830
The United States has 23 miles (37 km) of railroad.

October 26, 1825

The Erie Canal is completed. Measuring 363 miles (584 km) long, it connects the northeastern United States to the Great Lakes.

July 4, 1828

Work begins on the Baltimore & Ohio, the first U.S. railroad to offer service to the public.

1833

At 136 miles (219 km), the South Carolina Railroad becomes the longest railroad in the world.

1839

Kirkpatrick Macmillan, a Scottish blacksmith, invents the first pedal bicycle.

1833

It takes only seven hours to travel from Philadelphia, Pennsylvania, to New York City by train. The trip used to take three days by horse.

April 1838

The *Sirius* becomes the first ship to cross the Atlantic Ocean under steam power alone. The trip takes 18 days.

BY LAND AND BY SEA

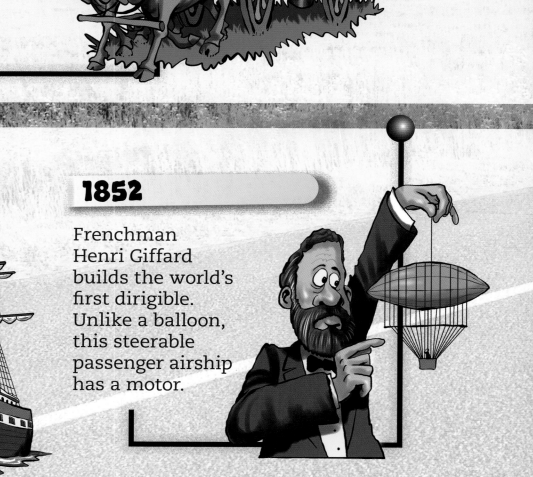

1841

The first wagon train of U.S. settlers begins the journey from the Missouri River to the Pacific Ocean.

1845

The steamship *Great Britain* is finished. It's the first ocean ship made of iron, rather than wood.

1852

Frenchman Henri Giffard builds the world's first dirigible. Unlike a balloon, this steerable passenger airship has a motor.

1858

The first stretch of asphalt is laid on a street in Paris, France.

January 10, 1863

The world's first subway opens in London, England. Called the Metropolitan Line, it uses trains powered by steam.

UNDERGROUND

1858

George Pullman introduces the Pullman sleeping car. Train passengers can now sleep in beds during overnight travel.

1860

The United States has more than 30,000 miles (48,280 km) of railroad track. That's more than the rest of the world combined.

1859

Etienne Lenoir builds the first practical internal combustion engine. This engine will help start the Automotive Age.

PAVING THE WAY

1865

The first concrete pavement is laid in Inverness, Scotland.

First Concrete Pavement

1871

English inventor James Starley patents a bicycle with one large and one small wheel. It's nicknamed the "Penny Farthing."

April 29, 1869
Central Pacific workers build 10 miles (16 km) of track in one day.

November 17, 1869
The Suez Canal opens. It connects the Mediterranean and Red Seas, shortening the journey from Europe to Asia.

May 10, 1869

The Central Pacific and Union Pacific Railroads meet at Promontory Summit, Utah. The first U.S. transcontinental railroad is completed.

August 2, 1873

CLANG! CLANG!

A cable car is tested on the steep hills of San Francisco, California. The car is dragged on rails by a long cable under the street surface.

1885

Gottlieb Daimler of Germany invents the first gas-powered motorcycle.

1883

To simplify train schedules, railroads in the United States and Canada replace local times with standard time zones.

1885

The Canadian Pacific Railway is completed. It's the first transcontinental railroad across Canada.

THE AUTOMOTIVE AGE BEGINS

July 3, 1886

Karl Benz, a German engineer, builds the first useful, gasoline-powered car in the world. It has three wheels.

1888

The first city-wide system of electric streetcars in the United States begins running in Richmond, Virginia.

1893

Brothers Charles and Frank Duryea build the first gasoline-powered car in the United States.

1896

German inventor Gottlieb Daimler builds the world's first truck.

Luigi's MOTORIZED trucking company (NO Horses!)

1898

John Holland, an Irish-American engineer, builds the first modern submarine.

September 1, 1897

The first public subway in the United States opens in Boston, Massachusetts. It's 1.5 miles (2.4 km) long.

1897

Francis E. and Freelan O. Stanley, twin brothers, produce the Stanley Steamer. It is the first commercial steam-powered car built by Americans.

UP, UP, AND AWAY!

1903

The Harley-Davidson Motor Company sells its first motorcycle. In less than 20 years, it will be the world's largest motorcycle manufacturer.

December 17, 1903

Wilbur and Orville Wright fly the first airplane at Kitty Hawk, North Carolina.

He's Orville →

← He's Wilbur

UPTOWN ←

DOWNTOWN →

A TRAIN

N TR

Tickets 5¢

October 27, 1904

The New York City Subway opens. The largest in the United States, it's 9.1 miles (14.6 km) long, with 28 stations.

October 1, 1908

The Ford Motor Company rolls out the first Model T. The car opens the way for the average person to buy an automobile.

1913

Henry Ford starts the first assembly line. Cars and other goods can now be made more quickly.

June 14, 1919

John Alcock and Arthur Brown make the first nonstop flight across the Atlantic Ocean. They fly from Newfoundland, Canada, to Ireland.

April 15, 1912
The RMS *Titanic* sinks in the North Atlantic Ocean.

New York

San Francisco

1920
About 1.2 million people travel by rail this year in the United States, an all-time record.

October 31, 1913

The Lincoln Highway opens. It's the first road to cross the entire United States.

August 15, 1914

The Panama Canal opens. It is a huge time-saving shortcut for ships traveling between the East and West coasts of the United States.

CONTROLLING THE SKIES

▶ May 20, 1927

Charles Lindbergh, an American pilot, flies nonstop across the Atlantic Ocean. He starts in New York and lands in Paris, France.

June 17, 1928

American pilot Amelia Earhart becomes the first woman to fly across the Atlantic Ocean.

1929

Greyhound Bus Lines begins service in the United States.

1933

Germany begins construction of a system of divided freeways called *autobahns*. These freeways become the model for U.S. interstates.

ACHTUNG! BERLIN 15 KM

1939

Igor Sikorsky, a Russian engineer, creates the first practical helicopter. It will be the model for all future helicopters.

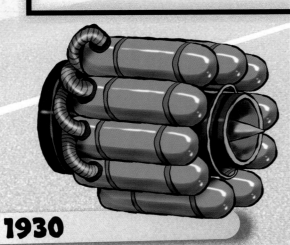

1930

Englishman Frank Whittle patents a design for an engine that will later power jet airplanes.

1938

Bohemian engineer Ferdinand Porsche designs the Volkswagen Beetle.

February 8, 1933

The first modern passenger airplane, the Boeing 247, begins service.

MOVING FARTHER, FASTER

1940

The first U.S. expressways open to traffic. They are the Merritt Parkway in Connecticut and the Pennsylvania Turnpike.

May 2, 1952

The world's first jet airplane begins commercial flights. It goes from London, England, to Johannesburg, South Africa.

February 10, 1942

Ford Motor Company stops production of all non-military vehicles as the United States enters World War II (1939–1945).

October 14, 1947

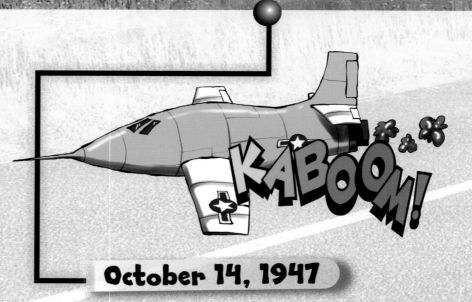

American pilot Charles "Chuck" Yeager makes the first faster-than-sound flight.

June 29, 1956

U.S. President Dwight Eisenhower signs the IHS Act into law. It creates the country's Interstate Highway System.

1959

The St. Lawrence Seaway opens to boats. The waterway runs from the Atlantic Ocean to the Great Lakes.

August 1, 1952

The first Holiday Inn opens. The start of motel chains is a sign of Americans' growing love for car travel.

1957

For the first time in history, more Americans travel by air this year than by rail.

October 4, 1957

The Soviet Union launches the world's first artificial satellite. Called *Sputnik* 1, it marks the start of the Space Age.

BLASTING INTO SPACE

September 30, 1968

Boeing rolls out the Boeing 747 "jumbo jet." It will be the world's largest passenger airplane until 2005.

▶ April 12, 1961

Soviet Yuri Gagarin becomes the first human to orbit Earth. He rides aboard the *Vostok 1* spacecraft.

June 16, 1963

Valentina Tereshkova, from the Soviet Union, becomes the first woman to fly in space.

October 1, 1964

Japan's "bullet train" becomes the world's first high-speed passenger train. It runs between Tokyo and Osaka. Travel time is cut from 6 hours, 30 minutes to 3 hours, 10 minutes.

March 2, 1969

The Concorde makes its first flight. The French-British supersonic airplane travels at more than twice the speed of sound.

May 1, 1971

ALL Aboard!

Amtrak is created in the United States. The government-run train system takes over passenger traffic from private railroads.

July 20, 1969

U.S. astronauts Neil Armstrong and Edwin "Buzz" Aldrin become the first humans to safely land on the moon.

UNITED STATES

DEVELOPING NEW TECHNOLOGY

November 14, 1994

The Channel Tunnel opens. Called the "Chunnel," the underwater tunnel allows train travel between England and France.

PLEASE rOLL UP yOur WiNdoWS!

Next 50 KM Under Water

April 12, 1981

The United States launches the space shuttle *Columbia*. It is the world's first reusable spacecraft.

July 7, 1981

The *Solar Challenger* crosses the English Channel. It's the first solar-powered aircraft.

1998

Driverless trains start running in part of the Paris subway. They're operated by computers.

1984

Americans Greg Johanson and Joel Davidson create the first 100-percent solar-powered car.

2000

Toyota releases the Prius. The car is the first four-door, gas-electric hybrid in the United States.

April 27, 2005

The Airbus A380 makes its first flight. It can carry up to 555 passengers, making it the world's largest airplane to date.

2011
Electric vehicles (EVs) become more widely available around the world.

December 31, 2002

The first magnetic levitation (maglev) rail line opens in Shanghai, China. Trains glide above tracks, moved by magnets.

June 21, 2004

SpaceShipOne makes the first manned private space flight. It is a test flight for a contest called the X PRIZE.

BUILD YOUR OWN TIMELINE

A timeline shows a number of events in chronological order—the order in which they happened in time. Make a timeline of the history of air transportation. Start with the Wright Brothers' success at Kitty Hawk in 1903 and end with today.

Use dates from this book as a starting point. Then search online for more dates by entering "history of flight," "history of flying," or "aviation history." Check out books in your local or school library. If you need help finding information, be sure to ask a librarian.

December 17, 1903

He's → Orville

He's ← Wilbur

?

?

TODAY

Glossary

asphalt—a black tar mixed with sand and gravel to make roads

canal—a channel dug across land; canals connect bodies of water so ships can travel between them

commercial—having to do with business

concrete—a mixture of cement, water, sand, and gravel that hardens when it dries

expressway—a wide highway with few stops that is used for high-speed travel

hybrid—a mixture of two different types

launch—to send off

lock—a "step" that carries a ship up or down between two water levels

locomotive—an engine that moves on its own power

mode—a method or way

orbit—to circle around an object

patent—to own the sole rights to make or sell a product

pave—to cover a road with a hard surface

pavement—the hard covering for a street or sidewalk

satellite—an object that orbits a planet or other space object

transcontinental—crossing a continent

transport—to move from place to place

TO LEARN MORE

More Books to Read

Bozzo, Linda. *Getting Around in the Past, Present, and Future.* Imagining the Future. Berkeley Heights, N.J.: Enslow Publishers, 2011.

Curlee, Lynn. *Trains.* New York: Atheneum Books for Young Readers, 2009.

Perritano, John. *Revolution in Transportation.* It Works. New York: Marshall Cavendish Benchmark, 2010.

Internet Sites

FactHound offers a safe, fun way to find Internet sites related to this book. All of the sites on FactHound have been researched by our staff.

Here's all you do:

Visit *www.facthound.com*

Type in this code: 9781404866614

Check out projects, games and lots more at
www.capstonekids.com

INDEX

Look for all the books in the series:

An Illustrated Timeline of Inventions and Inventors

An Illustrated Timeline of Space Exploration

An Illustrated Timeline of Transportation

An Illustrated Timeline of U.S. States